THE M[ORALITY OF] W[OMAN]

AND OTHER ESSAYS

BY

ELLEN KEY

TRANSLATED BY

MAMAH BOUTON BORTHWICK

THE MORALITY OF WOMAN
(TRANSLATED FROM THE SWEDISH)

"The law condemns to be hung those who counterfeit banknotes; a measure necessary for the public welfare. But he who counterfeits love, that is to say: he who, for a thousand other reasons but not for love, unites himself to one whom he does not love and creates thus a family circle unworthy of that name—does not he indeed commit a crime whose extent and incalculable results in the present and in the future, disseminate far more terrible unhappiness than the counterfeiting of millions of banknotes!"

C. J. L. ALMQUIST.

The simplest formula for the new conception of morality, which is beginning to be opposed to moral dogma still esteemed by all society, but especially by women, might be summed up in these words:

Love is moral even without legal marriage, but marriage is immoral without love.[6]

The customary objection to this tenet is that those who propose it forget all other ethical duties and legitimate feelings in order to make the sex relationship the center of existence, and love the sole decisive point of view in questions concerning this relationship. But if we except the struggle for existence—which indeed must be called not a relationship of life but a condition of life—what then can be more central for man, than a condition decreed by the laws of earthly life—the cause of his own origin? Can one imagine a moment which penetrates more deeply his whole being?

That many men live content without the happiness of love, that others after they attain it seek a new end for their activity, proves nothing against the truth of the experience that for men in general the erotic relation between man and woman becomes the deepest life determining factor, whether negatively, because they are deprived of this relation or because they formed it unhappily; or positively, because they have found therein the fullness of life.[7]

The depreciation for mankind of the significance of the sex relation and of the significance of love in the sex relation brings into it all the immorality still imposed by conventionalism as morality.

We no longer consider, as in our mother's youth, ignorance of the side of life which concerns the propagation of the race the essential condition of womanly purity. But the conventional idea of purity still maintains that the untouched condition of the senses belongs to this conception. And it would be right, if the distinction were made between purity and chastity. Purity is the new-fallen snow which can be melted or sullied; chastity is steel tempered in the fire by white heat. For chastity is only developed together with complete love; this not only excludes equally all partition among several but also makes a separation between the demands of the heart and the senses impossible. The essence of chastity is, according to George Sand's profound words: "to be able never to betray the soul with the senses nor the senses with the soul" ("de[8] ne pouvoir jamais tromper ni l'ame avec les sens ni les sens avec l'ame"). And as absolute consecration is its distinctive mark, so is it also its demand. This alone is the chastity which must characterize the family life and form in the future the basis of foundation for the happiness of the people.

Literature was, therefore, wholly justified when in the name of nature it attacked the hyperidealistic subtlety which raised the love of the heart to the highest rank and made that of the senses the lowest; and when it desired that the woman should not only know what complete love was but that she should also when she loved desire that completeness.

Because from time to time powerful voices were raised, like George Sand's or Almquist's, calling without consideration not only that marriage immoral which was consummated without mutual love but also that marriage immoral which was continued without mutual love—a purer consciousness has awakened in questions regarding the conditions of the genesis[9] of the unborn race and elevated the conditions of the personal dignity of man and woman. So eventually it will come to pass that no finely sensitive woman will become a mother except through mutual love; that this motherhood sanctioned legally or not so sanctioned shall be considered the only true motherhood, and every other motherhood untrue. Thus will mankind awaken to such a feeling of the "Sanctity of the generation," and to such an understanding of the conditions of the health, strength and beauty of the race, that every marriage which has its source in worldly or merely sensual motives, or in reasons of prudence or in a feeling of duty shall be considered as Almquist calls it: "A criminal counterfeiting of the highest values of life." And the same criminal counterfeit obtains in every married life which is continued under the compulsion, the distaste or the resignation of one of the two. Man will be penetrated with the consciousness that the whole ethical conception which now in and with marriage gives to a husband or a wife[10] rights over the personality of the other, is a crude survival of the lower periods of culture; that everything which is exchanged between husband and wife in their life together, can only be the free gift of love, can never be demanded by one or the other as a right. Man will understand that when one can no longer continue the life in love then this life must cease; that all vows binding forever the life of feeling are a violence of one's personality, since one cannot be held accountable for the transformation of one's feeling. Even though this new moral ideal should in the beginning dissolve many untrue marriages and thus cause much suffering, yet all this suffering is necessary. It belongs to the attainment of the new erotic ethics which will uplift man and woman in that sphere where now the spirit of slavery and of obtuseness under a holy name degrade them; where social convention sanctions prostitution alongside monogamy, and vouchsafes to the seducer but not to the seduced, social esteem, calling the unmarried woman ruined who in love has[11] become a mother, but the married woman respectable who without love gives children to the man who has bought her!

The erotic-ethical consciousness of mankind cannot be uplifted until the new idea of morality with all its consequences is clearly established.

This ideal has two types of adversary. One is the adherent of the conventional morality; the other the supporter of the transitory union to which the name of "free love" is erroneously applied.

Those of the first type demand quite the same morality for the man as for the woman. They assert that celibacy for either sex brings with it serious difficulties. They maintain that the social feeling of duty, not mutual love, must be the ground of conjugal fidelity. They call "pure love" love untouched by all that which they call "sensuality."

These same moral dogmas in recent years have manifested themselves in the effort to quench all fire, whiten all burning red coals, and drape all nudity in literature and art. The supporters of this dogma[12] certainly understand—since, to begin at the beginning they have surely glanced into the Bible and Homer—that the undertaking would be too vast were it to extend to classic literature. But all the more ardently they have directed their zeal against modern literature and art. And if they do not encounter energetic opposition the fig leaf will soon among us also attest the fall of taste and of the soul.

"Free love" has also its fanatics who are guilty of quite as crass excess. They have no conception of soulful and true devotion, which they consider an absurdity or a conventionality under which human nature cannot bow without hypocrisy. For since experience shows that lifelong love is frequently an illusion, so, they say, one must not begin by expecting it! The so-called Bohemians have shown as great monomania in their rotation around this one point, the right of the senses, as have the zealots of traditional morality in their rotation around their point, the suppression of the senses. The extreme result of both would be retrogression to a lower[13] degree of culture; in one case to the asceticism of the Middle Ages, in the other to the promiscuity of the savage. Both forget the reality of life. On the one side they ignore this reality in their absolute demands without consideration of temperament or circumstances; in their assertion of the unqualified moral superiority of woman and in depreciation of the significance of love for the full harmony of man and woman. On the other side they ignore this reality when they try to make woman as unrestrained morally as man has hitherto been; when they forget all the suffering of the new generation born and reared in such an unrestrained existence; when they learn nothing of the nature of woman from the many younger and older women who live solitary and yet sound and useful lives in the deep conviction that, since they have not found the great, mutual love, which decides existence, any union with a man would be degrading and unhappy. Development has, because of multifarious influences made entirety and continuity in love a greater life necessity[14] for the woman of culture in general than for the man of the same intellectual level. A man, therefore, ordinarily dissolves an erotic relation without bitterness when he has ceased to love, while a woman, even after her love has ceased, often suffers because the relationship has not endured a lifetime.

It is this ever increasing peremptory demand for erotic completeness of the woman of developed individuality of the present time, which causes her always to wish to more fervently cherish the personality of the man as entirely as it is her happiness and her pride to be able to give her own. It is this demand for entirety which, among Germanic peoples, at least, makes woman neither desirous nor psychologically fitted for the so-called "free love." This is evidently to be concluded from the vicissitudes of those who have tried it.

"Free love" is moreover quite as senseless an expression as "legal love." Because no external command can call love into being or repress it; it is in this sense[15] always free, yet as are all feelings, it is bound by certain psychological laws. If not, then it does not deserve the name of love. It is with love as with the human face: though the individual varieties are infinite, yet there are certain general characteristic features which make all these different faces human faces, all these different feelings human love. And in every time there is a type for both, which is recognized as nobler than the others.

This noblest type of love has been portrayed by a Danish writer,[A] who endeavored to show that a conception of life founded upon evolution need not lead to laxity in sexual relations. He shows how the erotic feeling, as all other feelings, has been developed from an incoherent, indeterminate and indefinite condition to one more coherent, determinate and differentiated, and so from a simple instinct for reproduction of the species has been finally [16]transformed to an entirely personal, inner love. The highest type of this love is that which exists between a man and a woman of the same moral and intellectual level; which demands of necessity reciprocal love in order to be perfected, and can therefore be contented with no other kind of reciprocal love than a corresponding erotic love. This perfect love includes the yearning desire of both lovers to become entirely one being, to free each other and to develop each other to the greatest perfection. If love is perfected and consummated thus by the life together, then can it be given to only one and only once in a lifetime. This thought of the Danish writer is expressed with the concise brevity of the poet, by Bjornson, when he says of the sensation "feeling oneself doubled" in the beloved one: "*That* is love, all else is not love." This feeling which liberates, conserves and deepens the personality, which is the inspiration to noble deeds and works of genius, is the opposite of the ephemeral, merely sensual love, which enslaves, dissipates and lessens the personality.[17]

[A]See Viggo Drewsen: "En Livsanskuelse grundet paa Elskow" ("A Conception of Life Founded upon Love") and "Forholdet mellem Maud og Kvinde belyst gjennem Udviklingshypothesen." ("The Relation between Man and Woman in the Light of the Hypothesis of Evolution.")

It is only the great love which has a higher right than all other feelings and which can establish its right in a life.

He who considers this love decisive for the morality of such an erotic union cannot believe that external ties are necessary to give ethical value to this union. Social considerations, prudence and feeling for others can indeed in certain cases make the legal bond desirable. But it can just as little give increased consecration to real love, as it can give any consecration whatever to a relation in which this content is lacking. And even if it would be too dogmatic to establish just the highest type of love as ethical norm for all relations between man and woman, since life proves that the highest love is still as rare as the highest beauty, yet it is on the contrary not premature to assert that this love, legally sanctioned or not, is moral, and that where it is lacking on either side, a moral ground is furnished for the dissolution of the relationship. The ever clearer consciousness that love can dispense with marriage yet marriage cannot dispense[18] with love, is already partially recognized in modern society, by the facility of divorce. And it is only a question of time when the law which gives to one person the power to constrain the other to remain with him against his will, will be abrogated, so contrary is this possibility to that developed conception of the freedom of love—which is not at all the same as so-called "free love!"

It is not historically true that it was, as has been asserted, some certain conception of morality, some certain form of concluding or dissolving marriage which, in the last analysis, has been a decisive factor in the progress or decadence of peoples. Among the Jews as among the Greeks, among the Romans as among our Germanic forefathers, at the most flourishing period, there existed many laws and customs which were considered moral that the present time considers immoral. The decisive thing for the sound life of these peoples was, that that which they considered right had sovereign power to bind them: the faithfulness to the conception of[19] duty more than the content of conception determines the moral soundness of a people. Society is in danger, not when the ideals are raised but when they are lost. But a very highly developed historical sense is necessary to see at the same time the connection and the difference between dissolution and reorganization. Moreover it is necessary to have the large view of the essentials of life which distinguishes the true poet, the view which Sophocles possessed when he let his Antigone follow the higher law of affection and commit a violation of the law which—according to the conception of that time—would lead to general license if it remained unpunished. The new ideal of marriage is now being formed in and through all the many literary and personal dissensions in which it constitutes the theme. Yes, it is formed also in the midst of all the conflicts of life for which marriage gives so much occasion. It is true there are now married people who separate because from the very beginning they considered fidelity impossible and so did not even strive for it. But[20] many other divorces have far more complex, psychological reasons. When two people are married young, personal development takes often entirely opposite directions; if they have married in more mature years, then their individual differences, already strongly marked from the beginning, make the problem of common life together difficult of solution. The strongly developed sensibility of the modern individual to disposition, nuances, variations of humor, makes a lack of sympathy still more unendurable; a true sympathy a far greater source of joy. The whole multiplicity of psycho-physical influences and impressions which the members of a family exercise upon one another for pleasure and displeasure, sympathy and variance, harmony and discord, are now in all relationships, but above all in marriage, felt with greatest intensity. It is in those natures most individually developed, most refined, for whom the nuances of the married life, not its simple primal colors, signify happiness or unhappiness.

To this general delicacy of feeling there[21] is added especially the heightened sensibility of woman to the discord between that which she expected in marriage and that which in reality it offered her, because the union often lacked the freedom, the understanding which her sympathetic feeling now craves. This lack of harmony is inevitable since the forms of marriage have not even approximately undergone the transformation which would correspond to the individual development of the two beings, of the woman especially, whom it unites. But while all these reasons, cursorily indicated here, contribute their part in the increased number of divorces, the life of finer feeling creates, on the other hand, an ever more intimate married life. There are married people who have pledged each other at marriage full freedom to dissolve the union when either of them so wished, and others who have never given legal form to their marriage yet realize fully and richly love in "sorrow and in joy," in sympathetic work together, in reciprocal, true devotion. There have been, on the other hand, cham[22]pions of so-called "free love" who were themselves by nature such pronounced believers in only one marriage that their life was wrecked when the one to whom they had bound themselves applied to their own case their own theories. It is always the character which ultimately decides. Character can make the radical theorist a moral paragon and the pillar of society resting upon conservative ground a reed of passion; it can make the advocate of egoism sublimely devoted and the apostle of Christianity deeply egoistic in his love.

So many men, so many souls; so many souls, so many destinies. And to wish to apply to this whole, complex, manifold, incalculable erotic life, with its unfathomable depths, an immutable ethical standard, when judging the relationship between man and woman, and to make this standard decisive also for the ethical value of the personality in other respects—is quite as naive as the attempt of a child to draw up in his little bucket the wonderful depth of the vast storm-driven sea.[23]

Love, as life, will fortunately remain an eternal mystery which no science will be able to penetrate and which reason cannot rule. Our only hope for the future is that man, endowed with a more delicate sense, will listen to the secrets of his own life. A more highly developed and differentiated soul life will give him a surer instinct or a keener power of analysis which will prevent him from confounding a passing sentiment of sympathy, need of tenderness or satisfaction of vanity with a love which decides existence. Now, on the contrary, many believe that a wave of admiration, of gratitude, or of pity is the whole sea; that the reflection of the fire of another is the holy fire itself!

No one can with certainty predict the final result of the profound revolution of the feeling and of the customs which is now taking place. But one thing appears certain: the danger to the future of mankind can scarcely be that the new ideal will result in general license. Rather it will lead to so individual, differentiated and refined love that erotic happiness will be[24] increasingly difficult to find and the idealists of love will more frequently prefer celibacy to a compromise with their greater demands for sympathetic love.

The occasional experience, often only the dream of such a love, sensible to the finest shades of the soul, to the most delicate vibrations of the senses—of a love which is an all comprehensive tenderness, an all embracing intimacy—has already raised the erotic demands and the erotic existence of thousands of men and women to a sphere of more infinite longing, more fervid chastity than that of their contemporaries. It is this experience or this dream which has already begun to assume form in the art and literature of the present time. It is true the extreme discord between the peculiar character of man and of woman has long been the favorite theme, especially in modern literature. But among the wild, discordant tones a new leitmotiv resounds which will swell and rise and fill the void with a harmony, still but faintly divined.

One of the conditions that this harmony[25] become as perfect as possible is that woman in life as in literature shall begin to be more honest and man more eager to listen when she reveals to him something of her own nature. Men have desired and justly that women should learn from their confessions in regard to the conflict between man and woman. But woman because of the conventional conception of womanly purity has been intimidated from conceding to man a deep insight into her erotic life experiences.

Only when women begin to tell the truth about themselves will literature universally illuminate the still unknown depths of woman's erotic temperament. To the present time it has been almost exclusively men poets who have made revelations about women. The nearer these poets have approached life, the more surely have they seen the highest expression of the eternal feminine as the great women poets also saw it: in erotic love and in mother love. And it was the completeness of her consecration which was in their eyes a woman's supreme chastity.[26]

It is the great poets who have taught and have continued to teach youth to revere the "all powerful Eros."

This is the only "morality" which has a future. Only by conforming to this shall we gradually succeed in preventing the erotic feeling from appearing sometimes as a brutal instinct or marriage from being founded upon a fleeting attraction.

An ideal of negative purity—even incarnated in the person of Jesus—cannot inflame youth and therefore cannot in the long run protect him. That alone which has the power not only to restrain but also to transform the brutal instinct is a conception of the existence of a higher feeling which belongs to the same sphere of life as the instinct itself.

To burn the ideal of a great love into the soul of youth in letters of fire—that is to give him a real moral strength. Thus there springs up in man the ineradicable, invincible instinct that an erotic relation can exist only as the expression of a reciprocal all comprehensive love. Thus will youth learn to consider the love-marriage[27] as the central life relation, the center of life, and he will be inflamed with the desire to develop and to conserve body and soul for the entrance into this most holy thing in nature, wherein man and woman find their happiness in creating a new race for happiness. Thus will young men and women in increasing numbers understand that their own happiness, as well as that of the coming generation will be the greater the more completely they can give their personality to love. Boys and girls, young men and maidens, men and women by coeducation, by joint labor and comradeship will develop in one another that mutual understanding which will remove the enmity between the sexes, in which modern individualization—and the therewith increasing demands of the personality—has so far found its expression.

The usages of individual homes will be differentiated, instead of as now maintaining the same conventional forms for all families. After some generations so educated, under the influence of relationships thus arranged, we shall see mar[28]riages such as even now not a few are seen, in which not observation of a duty but liberty itself is the pledge that assures fidelity. Then will love be cherished as the most delicate, most precious thing in life; then will egoism and unselfishness attain a perfect harmony, because the husband and wife find happiness only in assuring the happiness of the other. That is the union which the Norwegian poet defines when he calls true marriage "a yearning quest after each other, an energetic cultivation, assertion of the personality, in order to be able to give one's personality; an ever increasing intimacy of understanding of each other; a union which the whole course of life will make more profound."

So prepared, the absolute human ideal will become perhaps a living reality; not as an isolated man, not as an isolated woman, but as a man and a woman who shall give to mankind a new religion—that of happiness.

Many indeed still doubt that marriage[29] can become this highest form of existence in life, in which the surrender of the ego and the self-seeking of the ego reach a perfect harmony. It is asserted that this ideal condition can be attained perhaps by exceptional people, but never by ordinary people, and that the morality of the latter can be kept sound only by legal and social restraint.

My belief, however, is that, just as the Children of Israel followed the pillar of fire, so ordinary men follow at a distance exceptional men, and in this way mankind as a whole advances. Ordinary men are just now determined upon certain conceptions which at the end of the previous century were not conclusive even for exceptional people. The marriage of reason, for example, is already considered ignoble by many. The authority of the parents is very seldom in evidence either to coerce the children into a marriage without love or to restrain them from it. Even the superficial erotic emotion of our day is serious in comparison with the shallow and frivolous or vulgar and cruel gallantry[30] of the eighteenth century. In the geological deposits of legislation and still more in those of literature we can study these risings of the levels of the erotic sentiments. So we are thereby convinced that the demands and conflicts of the exceptional men become gradually those of the ordinary men also, even though the ordinary men are always some generations behind the men who are stirred by new emotions, new conflicts, when the many have reached the problems which some decades before occupied only the few.

Certainly it may, under present imperfect conditions, often be a duty not to destroy the outward form of marriage for the sake of the children. But by no means can this duty be preached as universally binding. Only the individual himself can in each separate case determine the dissolution best, both for the children and for the married couple themselves, of a marriage which has fallen asunder within. When we consider the development in its entirety, the sooner people cease to sanction the present marriage the more fortu[31]nate it will be; for the sooner will the transformation be forced upon us by which marriage will maintain its permanence only from within. Only then will man be wholly able to have the experiences and to find the new, delicate means by which fidelity can be strengthened and happiness assured. But man will not seek this expedient so long as he can rely upon the power of legal right and social opinion to hold together that which love does not unify.

The ever increasing individualization of love indicates that monomarriage will doubtless remain the form of erotic union between man and woman. But this rule will have, in the future, as in the past, many exceptions, since the feelings can change. The conflicts which will thus arise will bring suffering as a consequence, but not the bitterness nor the contention which the property sense in marriage now so often occasions. The deep consciousness that love belongs not to the sphere of duty but only to that of freedom will cause the one who has lost the love of the other[32] to feel the same resignation before the inevitable, as if he were separated from the other by death.

And in cases where the individual is not capable of this resignation, then the law as well as custom shall make it impossible for the one to hold back the other against his will. Each of the twain shall be master of his own person and of his property, of his work and of his mode of life; the union shall in each especial case be arranged by the agreement of the individuals, and the law shall decide only the rights and duties of the husband and wife in regard to the children.

When in this way it shall come to pass that neither the husband nor wife shall have in outward sense, in external things, anything to gain or to lose by the consummation or dissolution of marriage, then only the erotic problem appears in all its seriousness.

Many mistakes, many caricatures, many tragic failures will naturally be the result of freedom. Great waves have great combers. A new principle cannot be put[33] into effect without bringing with it new mistakes. But we may, however, be convinced that the laws of life—to which belongs the law that suffering follows the misuse of freedom—will finally be able to bring everything within its right limits. Nothing indeed has occasioned more suffering as an indirect consequence than Christianity, and although Jesus knew that, yet he did not hesitate to give to mankind this new creative force which destroyed in order to create. But it is above all His ideality which His present followers lack, the great ideality which dares to believe in the might of the spirit rather than that of the form.

It is, therefore, quite natural that these Christians, the upholders of society, oppose the new ideal of morality with vain apprehensions. They believe that a woman whose conscious aim is "Self-assertion in self-surrender" will forfeit the immediate, fresh originality in this surrender. They believe marriage must be destroyed when the support of its development is no longer bond and injunction,[34] but is its own vital force. They believe morality will lose in the struggle if youth learns to consider the love between man and woman as the central condition of life. These, and a hundred similar apprehensions have all one and the same source.

This source is the Christian conception of life which has displaced the great, sound, strong conviction of antiquity of the holiness of nature. Mary was the "Virgin Mother;" Jesus, celibate. Paul regarded marriage as the lesser of two evils. Thus man first learned to regard the unmarried state as the higher and the married as the lower state. The result of the Christian conception of life then was that the sex relation was regarded in and for itself as unholy, human nature in and for itself as base and the earthly demand for happiness as the greatest egotism.

Therefore the Christian conception of life is now, since it has accomplished its great task of culture, the development of altruism—an obstacle to the unified conception out of which the happiness of mankind will finally develop.[35]

No one who thinks or feels deeply dreams that this happiness can be easily achieved. The consistent belief of monism in human nature can only gradually leaven life. And until then suffering will be for the majority the first result of freedom. Even for the few, to whom the relationships have already given happiness, must this be incomplete in the measure in which they feel sympathy with all the suffering about them. But above all is happiness rare because the genius for happiness is still so rare, is indeed on the whole the rarest genius. To possess it means to approach life with the humility of a beggar, but to treat it with the proud generosity of a prince; to bring to its totality the deep understanding of a great poet and to each of its moments the abandonment and ingenuousness of a child; it means to be able to enjoy wholly each present, immediate, joy and yet to be able to give up the incidental joy for the enduring one.

Happiness lies so far from man; but he must begin by daring to will it. It is this[36]courage which Christianity broke down when it directed the soul from the earth to eternity and gave to renunciation the highest place among ethical values. Through the *Revaluation of all Values*, which is now going on, happiness will receive this Place.

He who contends for the deepest of all ideas, Spinosa's idea, that "Joy is perfection," contends with certainty of victory, however solitary he may stand, however much of his heart's blood may be shed in the strife.

We live still in our inmost soul only by that for which we die. And all for which we have died will live when the time shall come in which all we ourselves have suffered signifies nothing for us, yet that for which we have suffered signifies everything for others.

[37]

THE WOMAN OF THE FUTURE

[38]

[39]
THE WOMAN OF THE FUTURE

There are phrases which charm like a song, and one of these phrases is: "The Woman of the Future."

This sings for me in the verse of a poet and a seer, whose name now shines with the radiance of the morning star, although during his lifetime it was sullied with defamation as that of an atheist and destroyer of society—because the luminous path of his thoughts appeared to the prejudices of his contemporaries as a blinding flash of lightning. His poet's vision revealed to him a new time in which women would be

"... frank, beautiful and kindAs the free heaven, which rains fresh light and dewOn the wide earth[40]From custom's evil taint exempt and pure;Speaking the wisdom once they could not think,Looking emotions once they feared to feel,And changed to all which once they dared not beYet being now, made earth like heaven."

This beautiful profile of the woman of the future, which Shelley has traced, floats before me when I attempt here to draw her portrait in more precise outlines.

The storm and stress period of woman and the new social and psychological formations thereby entailed must, indeed, extend far into the twentieth century. This period of conflict will cease only when woman within and out of marriage shall have received legal equality with man. It will cease when such a transformation of society shall have come to pass that the present rivalry between the sexes shall be ended in a manner advantageous to both and when finally the work of earning a livelihood as well as care of the household shall have received such form[41] that it will weigh less heavily than now upon the woman.

Toward the end of the twentieth century only could the type of the nineteenth century woman have reached its culmination and a new type of woman begin to appear.

My ideal picture of the woman of the future, and when one paints an ideal one does not need to limit one's imagination, is that she will be a being of profound contrasts which have attained harmony. She will appear as a great multiplicity and a complete unity; a rich plenitude and a perfect simplicity; a thoroughly educated creature of culture and an original spontaneous nature; a strongly marked human individuality and a complete manifestation of most profound womanliness. This woman will understand the spirit of a scientific work, of an exact search after truth, of free, independent thought, of artistic creation. She will comprehend the necessity of the laws of nature and of the progress of evolution; she will possess the feeling of solidarity and regard for the[42] interests of society. Because she will know more and think more clearly than the woman of the present, she will be more just; because she will be stronger, she will be better; because she will be wiser, she will be also more gentle. She will be able to see things in the ensemble and in their connection with each other; she will lose thereby certain prejudices which are still called virtues. Nevertheless she will remain the one who forms customs. But she will not seek her support in social convention; she will find it in the laws of her own being. She will have the courage to think her own thoughts and to investigate the new thoughts of her time. She will dare to experience and to acknowledge feelings which she now suppresses or conceals. Her full liberty of action and the complete development of her personality will render possible intrepid efforts for life, an energetic striving after an existence which shall conform to her own ego. And such an existence she will be able also to find with surer instinct than now. She will understand how to work with more[43]intensity, to rest with more intensity and with more intensity to delight in all immediate, simple sources of joy than the woman of the present is able to do. Thus in the new woman the feeling of life will be enhanced, her experience will be more profound; her soul life, her demands for beauty, her senses will be more developed and refined. She will be more sensitive, more delicately vibratory; she will therefore be able to be more profoundly happy and also to suffer more keenly than the woman of our time.

Thus the woman of the twentieth century will give new value to the life of society and to art, to science and to literature. But her greatest cultural significance remains, however, by means of the enigmatic, the instinctive, the intuitive and the impulsive in her own being to protect mankind from the dangers of excessive culture. In face of knowledge she will maintain the rights of the unknowable; in face of logic, feeling; in face of reality, possibilities; and in face of analysis, intuition. Woman will above all further the[44] growth of the soul, man that of the intelligence; she will extend the sphere of intuition, he that of reason; she will realize tenderness, he justice; she will triumph by audacity, he by courage.

The woman of the future will not only have learned much, she will also have forgotten much—especially the feminine as well as anti-feminine follies of the present time.

With her whole being she will desire the happiness of love. She will be chaste, not because she is cold, but because she is passionate. She will be reserved, not because she is bloodless but because she is full blooded. She will be soulful and therefore she will be sensuous; she will be proud and therefore she will be true. She will demand a great love, because she herself can give a still greater. The erotic problem, because of her refined idealism, will be extremely complicated and often almost insoluble. Therefore the happiness which she will give and experience will be richer, more profound and enduring than anything which up to the present time has been[45] called happiness. Many traits which belong to the wife and mother of today will probably be lacking in the woman of the future. She will remain always the beloved, the sweetheart, and only so will she become a mother. She will devote her finest and strongest forces to the difficult and beautiful art of being at the same time the beloved and the mother; her religious cult will be to create the supreme happiness of life. Because she will know and value the psychical and physical conditions of health and beauty she will choose the father of her children with clearer vision and deeper feeling of responsibility than at present; she will bear and rear sound and beautiful beings and she herself will possess greater attraction and longer youth than the woman of the present. She will charm all her life, because she will always beautify existence. But she will please only because, at every age, she will be wholly herself; and her imperishable youth, her most perfect beauty, she will reveal solely to him whom she loves. She will know that the charm of the soul[46] is the most profound; and out of the plenitude of her being she will create the eternal renewal of this charm, always unexpected and in infinitely nuanced expressions of her personal grace. By her mere presence she will remove the constraint of form and custom and will create varying expressions, elevated by her own nobility, for the family life, the public life and for society. She will probably speak less than the woman of the present time, but her silence and her smile will be more eloquent. She will give herself always directly and always with moderation, different and always constant, spontaneous and always exquisite. Her being will pour forth, brimming free and fresh, like the surge of the mountain torrent, but like this, dominated by a certain inner rhythm. However far she allows herself to go—in ecstasy of joy, in passion of tenderness, in delirium of happiness or in the frenzy of grief—yet she will never lose herself. She will be a multiplicity of women and yet always one, whether she plays and smiles or suffers and smiles; whether she beams with health or bleeds with mortal[47] wounds; whether she be imbued with and radiate repose or nervous intensity, joy or tears, sun or night, coolness or ardor.

 The woman of the future exists already in man's dreams of women, and woman fashions herself according to the dreams of man. The modern man's ideal of woman is not the masculine woman, but the revelation of the "eternal feminine" developed in all directions. This new type of woman has already gleamed forth here and there, not only in our time but in centuries passed. In the Middle Ages she wrote the letters of Heloise; in the Renaissance, Leonardo painted her as Mona Lisa; and in the eighteenth century she held the salon of Mlle. Lespinasse. In our century she wrote the love sonnets of Elizabeth Barrett Browning; she appeared upon the stage as Eleonora Duse—and as in a precious stone her being is crystallized by the poet's words with which Rahel's personality was epitomized: "calm yet emotionally vivid."[3]

[B]Footnote from French translation:—The reference here is to Rahel de Varnhagen. The citation is taken from the "Hyperion" of Holderlin, a German poet of whom mention is made apropos of Nietzsche, upon whom he had great influence.

[48]

[49]

[50]

THE CONVENTIONAL WOMAN

[51]

THE CONVENTIONAL WOMAN

Conventionality is the tacit agreement to set appearance before reality, form before content, subordination before principal. Its field in certain measure is "vogue" changing according to the idea of beauty of each new season. In deeper sense, however, a part of the sphere of conventionality coincides always with that of law and custom, and with the conception of the amount of self-control and self-sacrifice which every individual must impose upon himself for the common life with others. The further the evolution of humanity advances, the fewer are the fields to which the power of society over the thought, belief, mode of life and manner of work of the individual is restricted. More and more prevalent[52] becomes the conviction that all those forms of expression of the individual which do not interfere with the rights of others must be free. A great part of the work of culture of each new generation has consisted and still consists in clearing away great masses of conceptions of right dried up into conventionalism, dead rubbish which prevents the new germs from sprouting. In every period strong voices are heard which desire freedom from the prevailing customs, and right of choice for the individual conscience and temperament. In this ever-continuous struggle it is important to distinguish what are really still living conceptions of right from factitious conceptions, which form only a conventional obstacle to a more beautiful freedom, a deeper truth, a greater originality, a richer life content.

Yet it is not only old conventionalism which needs to be rooted out. In every faction, in every social circle are soon formed lifeless collections of prejudices, paltry motives, dependent customs. It is always the women among whom conven[53]tionalism reaches its acme. For conservatism, that deep significant instinct of woman, becomes also often a prop of conventionality. Women are as yet seldom sufficiently developed personally to distinguish, in that which they wish to cherish, the appearance from the reality, the form from the content; or if they do distinguish, they have as yet rarely the courage to choose the content and reality if the majority have declared for form and appearance!

15

In the literature of the last ten years and in part also among women there prevails, however, a strong opposition to conventionality. This opposition has been directed especially against the archaic ideal of woman, according to which renunciation is still considered the highest attribute of woman; and against the antiquated conception of morality which regarded love without marriage as immoral, but any marriage, even without love, as moral.

The women who adopted the new ideal—which a Norwegian poet strikingly defined as "Self-assertion in self-surrender." [54]"Affirmation of self in giving of self"—encounter now on the part of the modern woman's-rights advocates the same kind of conventional objection as in the fifties and sixties was directed against the then new ideal of the earlier woman movement.

The older emancipation movement advanced along the first line in the effort to establish the right of woman as a human being; that is, to give to woman the same rights as to man. The present movement purposes to assert the right of woman as an individuality; the absolute right to believe, to feel, to think and to act in her own way, if it does not interfere with the rights of others. Since the first end was a general one, the movement could in great part be made effective by collective work in attaining that end; the exposition of the independence of the individuality of woman, on the contrary, must be the personal concern of each single individual. This those women do not understand who still are working ever for the first end—the rights of woman as a human being. They do not understand that every woman[55] must receive, not merely her universal rights, as a member of the body politic, but also her entire individual rights as the possessor of a definite personality. The right to establish an ego independent of, and perhaps entirely at variance with, theories and ideals is at heart the point of struggle between the one or the other individual woman and the women representatives of the earlier era of the woman question.

The discovery that each personality is a new world—which in Shakespeare found its Columbus, a Columbus after whom new mariners immediately undertook new conquests—this discovery of literature has as yet only partially penetrated the universal consciousness, as a truth of experience. But the fact that it has made a beginning, that the conventional, inflexible conception of the nature of man and of the problems resulting therefrom is giving place to a relative and individual conception—this is above all to be ascribed to the thinkers and poets, in whom the conventional has its deadliest[56] foe; the recreative poets whose characteristic is deep appreciation of all primal forces of existence, of all essential elements of life. For although conventionalism in the form of the echo springs up also around genius, yet the creative genius itself is always a protest against conventionality in which any selfjustified life or art—conception has perished.

The poet who here in the North shattered with a blow the archaic conventional ideal of woman who sacrificed herself in all circumstances, was Ibsen when he sent Nora out away from her husband and children in order to fulfill the duties toward herself; when by means of "Ghosts" he etched into the moral consciousness the idea that a woman's fidelity to her own personality is more significant for the welfare of others as well as of herself than her fidelity to conventional conceptions of morality.

And Ibsen has always been the annunciator of the freedom under one's own responsibility which is the key to individualism. Long has man listened, only in[57] part has he understood. And no consciousness is in this respect more hermetically sealed than that of certain woman's rights advocates! That all women should have the same rights as men, this is all that they mean in their talk about the freeing of the woman's personality. They forget that the right to be what she wishes entails often for the woman, as for the man, the obligation to suppress that which she really is by nature and feeling. They forget that the personality has deeper claims than the right to work. They overlook the infinite variety of shades of feeling, thought and character which caused the demand of solidarity in opinions and actions, among the women active in the woman question, to degenerate into suppression of woman's individuality. Certainly it is true that united action is still necessary in order that woman may obtain the rights which she still lacks. But all compulsory mobilized action is here more dangerous than elsewhere; because for the advance of the woman question in the deepest sense it is essential precisely[58] that the different feminine individualities show their useful faculties as freely as possible in the different fields of activity.

The conventionality which is a menace in the woman question betrays itself, not only in exaggerated demands for solidarity, but also in the mode of treating the objections of the opposition. It reveals itself in the lack of comprehension of the fact that the woman question, particularly in what concerns the labor field, now intersects on all sides the path of the social question. It especially evinces itself in the inability to understand how the woman question, as it advances in its evolution, becomes more complex, and how thereby, ever greater difficulties arise in taking an absolute position in the questions connected with it.

It is necessary that woman's opportunities for culture be multiplied. But do all these measures of culture develop also the personality? Have we not met the finest, most original, most charming natures among unlettered dames of seventy and eighty years, or among such[59] women as never had a systematic education? It is right that the wages of women should be increased; but will the labor value of women increase in proportion? Can we even desire that the majority of these women bent over their desks shall devote a live interest to their work, when their sole essential being would first find expression only when bent over a cradle? It is well also for girls of wealth to wish to have a vocation. But is it also good if they, because they can be satisfied with a smaller wage, take away the work from poor girls and men, often more competent, who have to live entirely by the fruits of their work, and must therefore demand larger wages?

So long as these and many other questions remain unanswered, there is today quite as much that is conventional in rejoicing unreservedly over the many girls who become students or leave the home, where they are very much needed, for outside work, as there was in our grandmother's time in wishing to limit the province of woman to the kitchen, the nursery and the drawing room.[60]

It is not yet known whether woman, through the competition for bread, will develop physiologically and psychologically to greater health and harmony. Woman is a new subject for research, and only centuries of full freedom in choice of labor and in personal development can furnish material for well grounded conclusions. Many signs, however, point to this:—that an ineffaceable, deep-rooted psychological difference due to physical peculiarities will always exist between man and woman, which probably will always keep her by preference active in the sphere of the family, while he probably will remain active in other spheres of culture. But with a perfect equality with man and a full personal development, woman can have a significance for culture in its entirety and for the direction of society which we can still scarcely divine.

The conventional points of view, just mentioned in considering the woman question, retard the development of woman's individuality above all because they overlook the diversity of nature and[61] the complexity of the problem. The conventional conception of self-renunciation as the highest expression of womanhood is still continually the greatest obstacle to the achievement of woman's personality. To be able to perish for a loved being with joy is one of the beautiful inalienable priviliges of woman nature. But by considering this under all circumstances as ideal, woman has thus retarded not only her own development but also that of man. If we compare marriages of older generations with those of the younger, the men of the latter show great advance in regard to considerate tenderness and sympathetic understanding toward their wives—wives who have on the other hand a personal life more complete and with other demands than formerly. Both have thus gained since women have begun to practice the self-renunciation of self-assertion! Because for every self-sacrificing woman nature it is infinitely harder to take her due than to sacrifice it.

Conventional womanhood will ever[62] have its strongest support in education.

The individuality of a child is seldom repressed in the inconsiderate and brutal manner of former times. But by attrition it is effaced. In the olden times the children enjoyed a certain freedom in the nursery where the expression of life, manifestation of joy, pleasure and displeasure, sympathy and antipathy of the growing personality was not continually moderated. Now the children are continually with the parents and these accustom them to a certain exacting restraint. The children wish to be entertained; they cannot play of their own initiative, for they lose the desire that originates in the freedom of the creative phantasy. Neither children nor parents possess themselves in peace. In the continual association the children are worn out by commands so varied and numerous that obedience cannot be maintained. They do not, therefore, learn the discipline necessary for the development of their personality—to subordinate the unessential life expressions to the essential and to dominate even[63]over these last—a culture of the fallow child ground which must begin early in order to become a second nature.

And this happens only when the educator knows clearly what he will adhere to as essential in the development of the child, and when according to that he establishes his commands and prohibitions, which must be few in number but as immutable as the laws of nature, and if violated must bring upon the child, not artificial punishment, but the inevitable results of the act itself. So can man by fixed practice form the child of nature into a man of culture, who out of consideration for himself and for others curbs his tendencies which are inimical to society, without, however, suppressing his personality. For outside the field of immutable laws, children ought not to be constrained or coerced against their nature and their disposition, against their healthy egoism and against their especial tastes.

Now many mothers by their own effacement of self develop an unjustified egoism of the child, but desire in other respects a[64] self-control, a circumspection, a moderation and discretion such as a whole life has not ordinarily been able to inculcate in the mother herself. Out of this soft clay, which is material for an individuality, parents, servants and teachers mold a society being, sometimes a social being, but never a human being.

This modeling is called education. And a part of the earliest education must, as I have just shown, truly consist in that of molding. But after the first years of life the aim of education should be to prevent all molding and on the contrary to assure the freedom or development of the single force which, considered in the light of the whole, makes it significant for mankind that new generations succeed those which have disappeared—the force of a new personality.

Every child is a new world, a world into which not even the tenderest love can wholly penetrate. However openly the clear eyes meet ours, however confidingly the soft hand is laid in ours, this tender being will perhaps one day deplore the[65] suffering of his childhood, because we treated him according to the assumption that children are replicas, not originals; not new, wonderful personalities. It is true the child in certain measure is a repetition of the child nature of all times, but at the same time, and this in a far higher degree, an absolutely new synthesis of soul qualities, with new possibilities for sorrow and joy, strength and weakness.

This new being will, upon his own responsibility, at his own risk, live this terrifyingly earnest life. What creative force, new inceptions, he will be able to bring to it; what elasticity he will possess under the blows of destiny, what power to give and to receive happiness—all depends, outside of nature itself, in essential degree upon the educator's method of treating this individual child nature.

Goethe long ago lamented that education aspired to make Philistines out of personalities. And this is now much worse since education has become pedagogical, without at the same time becoming psychological.[66]

Only he who treats the feelings, will and rights of a child with quite the same consideration as those of a grown person, and who never allows the personality of a child to feel other limitations than those of nature itself, or the consideration, based upon good grounds, for the child's own welfare or that of others—only he possesses the first requisite principle of real education. Education must assuredly be a liberating of the personality from the domination of its own passions. But it must never strive to exterminate passion itself, which is the innermost power of the personality and which cannot exist without the coexisting danger of a corresponding fault. To subdue the possible fault in each spiritual inclination by eliciting through love the corresponding good in the same inclination—this alone is individual education. It is an extremely slow education, in which immediate interference signifies little, the spiritual atmosphere of the home, its mode of life and its ideals signify on the contrary almost everything. The educator must above all[67] understand how to wait: to reckon all effects in the light of the future, not of the present.

The educator believes often that he spares the child future suffering when he "opposes his onesidedness," as it is called. He does not reflect that in the effort to force the child in a direction contrary to that in which his personality evinces itself, he merely succeeds in diminishing his nature; yes, often merely in retaining the weakness in the quality, not the corresponding strength!

But ordinarily it is indeed no such principle, but only the old thoughtlessly maintained ideal of self-renunciation which is decisive. We repress the child's joy of discovery and check the spirit of enterprise;

wound his extremely sensitive sense of beauty; exercise force over his most personal possessions, his tokens of tenderness; combat his aversions and quench his enthusiasm. Amid such attacks upon their individual being, their feelings and their inclinations most children, but especially girls, grow up. It is therefore not[68] surprising that when grown they seldom look back upon their childhood as a happy time.

An intense feeling of life, a sense of plenitude, entirety, of the complete development of the powers of the potentialities—this constitutes happiness. Children have more possibilities of happiness than adults, for they can experience this feeling of joy of life more undividedly and immediately. They should utilize these possibilities of happiness while the parents have partial power over their life. Soon enough must they on their own initiative attempt, accomplish, bleed; and herein no one of all the influences of education has even approximately the significance of this: that the individual be not overtrained, that he have still strength enough to live. That means: to suffer his own sorrow, to enjoy his own happiness, to perform his own work, to think his own thoughts, to be able to devote himself absolutely and entirely—the sole condition of being able to work, to love and to die.

It is a deep psychological truth that the[69] kingdom of heaven belongs to the children. For no one attains the highest that life offers in any other way than by simplicity, unworldliness and the power of devoting his whole being without reserve to his object. This is the strength of the child nature. If a mother by education has preserved this holy strength and developed it to a conscious power, then she has given to mankind not only a new being but a new personality.

But the education in the family, just as in the school, is tending in the opposite direction. The destruction of the personality is therefore the great evil of the time.

Yet man is fortunately a vigorous organism. And those, whose personality has been bowed or repressed by education, could raise themselves again and create freedom for their development if they were aware of the value of this freedom.

Few beings and so likewise few women can be exceptional. But if only a few are destined for a great personality, yet nevertheless most can, in spite of the errors[70] of education, develop a certain degree of personality, if they are deeply, earnestly concerned in it.

For everything is interrelated. No one lives unpunished by a second hand. We cannot advance intellectually by borrowing, without becoming also morally less scrupulous. We are today unjust to a book, a picture, a drama, because we pronounce judgment upon it according to the words of others, or because we do not dare to show the pleasure it gives us, in case the critic has not granted us permission to be pleased, or because we feign indignation we do not feel, but which others require of us in the name of taste or morality. Tomorrow, in the same way, we shall be unjust or dishonest to man, or to our own feeling—an injustice or a dishonesty which can have influence over the destiny of a whole life.

The sum of spiritual riches, of spiritual utilities, is thereby diminished if we do not cede to the whole what is most essentially ours. That which is really our own may be great or small, rich or insignificant[71]—if we ourselves have felt or thought it, it is more significant to others than that which we merely repeat, even if our authority be the highest. And in those cases where we must rely upon authorities, we still can put a certain personality into our choice and honesty in acknowledging our indebtedness, by confessing that we have borrowed our judgment we can put honesty and originality into this dependence.

It is possible for no one to acquire more than a limited amount of the results of culture, to form an entirely original judgment oftener than in a few isolated cases. But each one can learn to understand that it is a mark of culture not to pronounce judgment upon questions with which he is not conversant. Good taste prescribes that just as one refuses to wear false jewels if one possesses no real ones, so one should refrain from pronouncing judgment upon persons or questions upon which one has not formed an opinion through one's own impressions. When this honesty begins to be considered a mark of spiritual refinement, then will the[72] culture of woman have made quite as great advance as when she learned to read. For next to the power to form decisions for one's self stands in culture value the ability to understand what opinions one does not possess and the courage to recognize one's delicacy.

Courage and truth—that is what women lack above all. And these are the qualities which they must cultivate if the feminine personality is to grow. This does not result because women devote themselves to study, be it ever so thorough, or to social tasks, be they ever so responsible. Both further the development of woman's personality in the measure only in which her own investigations, her own choice, make her means of culture and her work an organic part of herself. To develop woman's personality from within—that is the great woman question. To free woman from conventionality—that is the great aim of the emancipation of woman.

Such a conception of the woman question is for me the ideal conception of this[73]present great movement. And ideality does not mean to adopt as the conception of life that which the majority considers ideal. Ideality means to live for the ideal, which has inflamed our consciousness and not to violate this consciousness by adapting it to such ideals as we feel with our whole soul are lower.

If it is true that "the lack of genius is the lack of courage," so then is it still more true in regard to the lack of personality. Here lies one of the reasons why individuality is less often found among women than among men. A man is more fully inflamed with his idea, the object of his work; he is more intense in that which he knows and which he wills. He becomes thus often—just as the child—more onesided, almost always more egoistic, but much more absolute than a woman in like position. She is rarely, except in love, wholly penetrated by that which occupies her. It is then easier for her to be considerate, to look about continuously upon all sides. She is more mobile, more quickly sensitive, more manysided and more sup[74]ple than man, and therein lies her strength. But just as that of man, it is bought at the price of corresponding weakness. For equipoise is still so difficult in human nature that a good quality is often not the product of a multiplication, but is the remainder after a subtraction.

The man becomes thus especially creative through his greater courage to dare, his more intense power to will; the woman becomes the often anxious conservator. She cherishes with fidelity, not only the customs and memories of the home, but also society's traditional sentiments and conceptions of right. But this very conspicuous conservatism of the woman is exactly that which has obstructed the development of exceptional femininity.

The personal independence of man is hampered because he must work ordinarily in close association with others; whereby he is bound by party discipline and party spirit, by considerations for preferment or other interests.

The personality of woman on the other hand is more fettered by conventional con[75]ceptions of morality and a conventional ideal of woman. She will not distinguish the self-sacrifice which is of value from that which from all points of view is valueless. She does not rely upon her own instinct for right if this instinct deviates only a hair's breadth from the generally accepted idea. She pardons the one who sins against established conceptions of right, provided only he recognizes their validity; but she condemns the one who has acted contrary to this conception in sincere conviction, because his idea of right differs from that of the majority! She confounds in her judgment temperament and opinions, doctrine and life—a confusion which is the origin of all spiritual tyranny, of all social intolerance. Especially does this obtain in questions which concern the relation of the sexes. Every one who expresses an opinion at variance with the conventional ideal of morality has then incurred intrusive conclusions and blasting defamation of his private life. On the part of women then—if it is a question concerning a woman—it[76] must all the more be accepted that it requires not only a glowing red belief but also a snow-white conscience to dare defy society in its most sensitive prejudices.

Conventionality of the woman attains its culminating point in the thoughtless and conscienceless repetition of others' words by which most women lower their spiritual level, distort, disfigure their character and eventually stultify their personality.

A woman who makes any pretensions to fineness, evinces this among other things, by avoiding all borrowed or sham luxury. She scorns spurious effects, tinsel, and disdains therefore in her dress and her home all artificial ornamentation.

But this same woman utters boldly counterfeited opinions and spurious judgments as her own. Even if she possesses it she dare not express a fresh, original opinion, a warm direct feeling. And her forgeries are then transmitted by other plagarists from circle to circle. Thus "Public Opinion" is formed upon the most delicate life problems, the most serious[77] life work. Thus the most noble actions become dubious and the vilest calumnies positive authentic truths. Thus the air becomes congested with the grains of sand, under which a man's works of honor are buried.

But a work or a renown which has been interred can be exhumed. It is the blind re-echoers of others' words, themselves, who must at length disappear forever.

Made in the USA
Middletown, DE
05 November 2019